MW01089372

A very special thanks goes to our editor, Patti's sister, Deborah Wile-Taves. From the beginning she has shared our vision of providing hope and has guided us with each sentence and each paragraph of every story. Her skills as an editor abound, but her understanding for what we wanted to give the reader comes from her own story of loss and what it takes to find hope again. Thank you for coming on this journey with us. We could not have done this without you.

A special acknowledgement goes to Ande Lyons of Possibility Partners. One of our biggest cheerleaders who said, "Patti, there's a book in here, you need to do this." Her constant words of encouragement made us believe that we could. Thank you, "Muahs of Love"

Introduction

It is difficult to imagine surviving grief much less transcending it. Can you ever find emotional and spiritual peace? Do you feel you will ever be able to have HOPE in your life again and find meaning? Do you want to honor your loved one's memory and be inspired to do so?

On the following pages we hope you will be inspired by the personal stories of those who have been on their own grief journey, and who have found hope again. The photography, affirmations, and quotes will help you to navigate your own path to living a life of joy, gratitude and love.

Our passion has been for helping others who have experienced a loss simply by sharing our own stories. It has been important for us to be role models to those going through grief, and to show them that they need not to do this alone, and that they can find hope again. This book is another part of our journey.

"We need not to walk alone……

We reach out to each other with love and

understanding and with HOPE……

We come together from all walks of life,

from many different circumstances……

We need not walk alone."

We hope this book will be a positive piece of your journey……

Foreword

I have had the distinct privilege of knowing Patti Comeau-Simonson and Helen Cogan since 2006 and 2010 respectively, having met them both through my work at the Bertolon Center for Grief and Healing in Danvers, MA.

Over the years, in sharing with me the stories of their husbands, I have been moved, inspired and awed by what these two women have done with their experiences of grief, and how they have been transformed.

As a therapist specializing in the area of grief and loss, I have come to understand that the path one undertakes toward healing is not for the faint of heart. It is a strangely alchemical process, the transmutation of darkness into light. It's a hero's journey, a vision quest, yet one that no one asks for. It requires considerable courage, strength, heart and will, and the ability to feel the fear and keep going, flying blind, yet trusting that there will be something better on the other side of the abyss.

Although there is much about losing a loved one that is out of our sphere of control, an important realization is in choosing what we do with it. At worst we become resentful, embittered victims of life's perceived cruelty, contracting in on ourselves, convinced that the only possibility for our happiness died with our beloved. In choosing this reaction, we stop living as well. At best, we use it to gingerly, tentatively inch us toward our new lives, discovering over time new roads to joy, passions we never recognized within us, and unsung talents and skills that previously lay dormant. If we allow it, we are gently nudged forward in this endeavor by angels, seen and unseen, whispering encouragement, knowing for us what we can't yet know for ourselves. We can only hope and trust.

When we stand on the threshold of life after loss, this is our choice point.

This beautiful, inspirational book that you now hold in your hands is the co-creation of two women, authors Patti and Helen, who have chosen to say "yes" to the challenges of this life, answering the call and hearing what is theirs to do; crafting a precious gift for the world from the wisdom gained from their combined experiences, their journey from darkness to light.

I am grateful to them both for walking through the fire, and birthing this collection of amazing images and uplifting words gleaned from the ashes of grief.

It is my hope that the hands that touch these pages, and the hearts that are opened by them, find comfort and solace here.

~ Kelly Russell LMHC

Dedication

This book is dedicated to my "Hope Representatives" who have committed themselves to helping those who have experienced the loss of a loved one to find "hope" again. They have been the inspiration for me to continue sharing my journey with others through the **Hope and Healing with Peers** program and the making of this beautiful and very visual "**Book of Hope**". Thank you!

A special love-filled acknowledgement to all of my former colleagues, my friends, who have generously mentored me and who said a long time ago, "Patti, you should continue to share your story with those who are grieving". Thank you!

To the many members of my family who have traveled this journey with me. My sons Marc and Matthew who let me lean on them when they should have been leaning on me. To my brothers Mike and John who allowed me for a time to be their little sister instead of being the oldest, and to my beautiful sister Debby, who had experienced the loss of her own husband just a year and a half before me, but kept telling me we could be happy again if we just put it out there for the universe to hear. I love you…

To Helen Cogan, one of the most amazing women I have ever met! Your journey is filled with inspiration and courage, and you have shared it so graciously with those who are grieving. Your photography gives us all hope and I am filled with deep gratitude that we are collaborating on this loving endeavor together. You are the best!! Peace!

Finally, to my husband Rick. You put laughter back into my life and helped me to realize that my heart was big enough to love again. You have been a wonderful husband, and amazing grandfather, all the while helping me to keep David's memory alive. You have been a major part of my journey, encouraging me to share my passion in helping others to find HOPE again. I'm so glad you have been part of my story……I love you!

~ Patti Comeau-Simonson

Dedication

I am dedicating this book to those who believed in me before I believed in myself, who helped me realize that anything is possible when the passion for what you love exists in your heart and you are willing to take the risk to unearth it.

To my family, children and dearest friends. To the widows and widowers who shared their journeys with me.

To a few special people….Siobhan Mahoney, the facilitator of my first grief group who told me to find something I have always wanted to do but never made the time for. "Find your passion" she said. It is her words that opened my heart and soul to my camera which provided the conduit to my ongoing healing.

To Kelly Russell, my therapist. She walked me ever so gently through my journey of grief and continues to be a driving force in helping me see that I must trust my heart, and that life is ALL about gratitude.

To Patty Greeley. Widows we are, six months apart, two phone calls a day for the past five years. My BFF.

To Patti Comeau-Simonson who told me we could write this book and I believed her!

Most importantly to my late husband Bob whose death prompted all of this. I would give a gazillion dollars to have him here with me and NEVER have written this book…but that is not the way it is supposed to be. Until we meet again, I love you!

~ Helen Cogan

The Power of Hope

During your loss, you may have been so angry or despondent

that you blurted out a number of curse words,

including some four-letter ones. But there is another

four-lettered word that might serve you better at this time.

That word is "Hope"

Hope is the greatest treasure you have.

When all else fails, hope is something to hang on to.

Don't give up.

~ Allen Klein, Learning to Laugh when you feel like Crying

Embracing Life after Loss

HOPE is the shelter that keeps us safe in the storm.

H- is for holding the light in your heart, even if it only flickers very faintly in the beginning, that will warm to a bright glow over time to heal us and hold us.

O- is for opening our hearts and minds to let in and honor all that we feel: the sorrow, the anger, the guilt, the longing, the missing, the fear and giving ourselves permission to accept all our emotions with love, patience and understanding.

P- is for the peace that we feel is lost at times but that still occupies a special place in our hearts and souls where it always resides as the seed of our humanity.

E- is for the eternal energy of life, the force from which we sprang, and the pool of love that beckons us home.

HOPE waits for us in the shadows at the beginning of our suffering, but opens its arms to us through our friends, our families, our precious memories and our capacity for love.

~ Christine Silverstein, peer facilitator

His Shoes

I still have his shoes under my bed. I know he is not coming back, but it helps me feel close to him and gives me comfort.

Ronnie and I were married for 26 years. We were a normal, happy family. We had our son, our careers and the usual ups and downs. But we always had each other, we could always count on that.

And then he was gone. How did this happen? We are not supposed to die until we are old, right? He was an athlete, in excellent condition. He prided himself on being fit and healthy. People like that don't get leukemia do they? I want an answer but there is none.

When did this happen? One day I'm a happily married woman, and the next I am a widow, a single woman, on my own, paying the bills and writing the checks. I am alone and in shock.

We thought he had the flu. The symptoms were pretty clear, but blood tests proved otherwise. Before I knew it we were at a cancer hospital listening to the doctors explain the prognosis. We tried everything we could, even a bone marrow transplant. But the outcome was not what we hoped. Ronnie died one week before Christmas, and Christmas has never been the same. It's been five years and the emotions of loss and sadness begin to mount long before December 25th arrives.

I decided to go right back to work. I love my job and knew I had the support and help of my wonderful co-workers through those difficult first few months. Though they did whatever they could, the days felt endlessly long, especially the weekends. As I tried to establish a regular routine, I was confronted with the reality of Ronnie's absence at every turn. Each night I came home to an empty house where there was no one to ask me about my day, no one to cook dinner for, no one to cuddle with, and no one to say "I love you." The loneliness was palpable and I hated what my life had become.

When it seemed that the emptiness would swallow me up, a co-worker spoke to me about a Grief Center she knew about. It was the person on the phone whose words guided me to a whole new path, "I completely understand what you're going through. " Someone got it. Someone heard my pain and threw me a lifeline. Soon I was enrolled in an 8 week group made up of others like me who had recently lost a partner/spouse, and I also began individual counseling sessions.

What a difference those steps made to my life! After moving through those experiences I was asked if I would like to take an even bigger step, to train as a peer facilitator. It was a wonderful way to pay it forward. I was soon using my experiences to comfort and guide others going through loss.

All of this gave me an enormous amount of hope. I was not alone and I would get through it. Though Ronnie's death was unchangeable, I knew I had choices and it was my choice to find a different life where I could once again be happy and content.

Five years have passed since Ronnie's death and I have more good days than bad days. I can't change what happened, but I can choose which new paths I will follow and in which direction I will move. I now move forward with a heart filled with hope, love and enthusiasm for life.

The pain of Ronnie's death gets softer each day, and thoughts of him bring me comfort and a sense of gratitude for all the time we got to spend together. His shoes still remain under my bed, where I want them to be, close to my heart.

~ Patti Greeley

When Hope Took Hold

I can still vividly recall the moment I learned that my mother died. I remember the sound of the phone ringing as it woke me up, and trying to sound calm for the police officer on end of the line, and then dropping the phone and slipping to the floor because the the news had knocked the wind out of me, the expression on my friend's face when I told her in the parking lot as I left to drive home, what the sky looked like, what shirt I was wearing. My mother was killed instantly in a car accident an hour before I received the call. I remember the confusion I experienced trying to comprehend that she had actually died an hour earlier, when I was sleeping. I was planning to see my mom later that day after not having seen her for two months- my longest stretch to date- because I was heading home for spring break. That moment, and those days ahead, changed my life completely.

My mother, a single parent, died in March of my junior year of college. I managed to graduate due to stubbornness, not because I had any interest or attention span to focus on the work. It was as if someone dared me to finish college when I was least capable, when I could barely hold my attention to one thing for more than a minute, and by proving them wrong I would somehow bring some sort of control, something positive, back into my life. My anger about my loss propelled me to the end of my senior year. I moved back to my childhood home after graduating to take on the role of head-of-household. I worked a job, reconnected with some old friends and made some new ones, paid bills and monitored and worried about our old house's steadily declining condition. This life that I had chosen, returning home, was what I felt I was supposed to be doing. It was a reflection of my mother, a responsible person who took care of important things. I saw a therapist and tried counting my blessings. But I was drowning. I loved my mother so much that I wanted to preserve as much of her life, her belongings, her reputation, her home as I could. I tried staying in touch with her friends, and felt her presence when I was with them. But deep inside I knew that dedicating my life to my mother would not bring me peace or healing and after two years I knew I had to to get as far away as I possibly could.

I made the decision and moved into an apartment in Boston in August of 1999 on my 25th birthday. And that was the moment that hope took hold in my life. On that day I took a risk, considered all my options, and stepped into the unknown. I couldn't help but feel her hope in me, her excitement that I had reclaimed my life. My concern that I was leaving behind my efforts to preserve her life and spirit drastically shifted, and I found that I was doing just that by caring for myself. I was doing just that in remembering her priorities and choices and applying them to my life in a new place. I realized that our spiritual connection was going to be a strong and lifelong connection, and that I could move forward knowing she'd always be with me. And my memories of her became more frequent and comforting.

Two months later I met the man who would become my loving, compassionate, hilarious, understanding husband. A man I thought couldn't exist, who's done everything in his power throughout our relationship to ensure that I'm okay, and more recently, that our children are okay. A man my mother would have hand picked for me, and probably did. My mother would have embraced him like her own son. The image makes me smile every time I imagine it.

I think of my mother every day. I think of her face, her laugh, her comfortable way of just being with me. I wonder if she ever stared in wonder at me as I do at my own children after they say something incredibly sweet or funny. I laugh to myself thinking that it would have been so much fun to share some of the hilarious stories of my three children and their distinct personalities and compare them to her own funny stories about me. I think of how both she and I worked with the elderly at end-of-life, and wonder about her professional opinion on certain topics. It's funny how it's been almost 18 years since her death, and yet I consciously followed her example last night while caring for my sick child, and considered her opinion about a work issue earlier this week.

The pain of my loss did, in fact, lessen. Maybe it was the passage of time, or maybe it was forgiving myself for not staying home, or maybe it was settling into a new normal that turned out to include my mother's presence more than I ever anticipated. Life is unpredictable, and I'm so glad I can still rely on my mother through it all.

~ Siobhan Mahoney

"Hope is that quiet persuasive thing inside us that keeps us going when we no longer think we can."

Pat, peer facilitator

There is Always Hope

I never knew that grief could be so in-your-face all the time. I lost my husband on April 3, 2013 and it's the hardest thing I've ever gone through. It's the loneliness that's so hard. In the first year I've had days where I couldn't grasp not being with my best friend. It's as though my circle doesn't touch anymore…there's a space where he used to be. But as the journey continues, those days have mercifully turned into moments.

I have to remind myself that I'm not alone. My hope for others out there who are experiencing great loss is that they keep moving forward, find a place that feels safe, find a new comfort zone. That's what I have done. That's where my hope lies.

I gauge my growth on the journey by realizing all the small milestones I have reached. I do things today that I never thought I'd be able to do. Recently I went out to eat by myself at a restaurant. I was seated alone at the table and at first wondered self-consciously if people were looking at me. But then I told myself I didn't care and I felt better….another big step for me and I was proud of myself.

That first summer the mornings were hardest for me. That is when my husband and I would go for our daily coffee down the beach. There we would sit and talk, plan our day and just be together. Such an ordinary habit that we enjoyed so much. This summer, about a year and a half after his death I decided to take myself to the beach every Sunday morning with a cup of coffee. I was forming a new habit and finding comfort in the old one, and again I felt proud. I found myself thinking back to my happiest memories. My emotions came and went as gentle as the ocean waves, no longer the tidal waves they once were.

I pick myself up every day and say "That's one more day that I've made it through." Moving through this grief is my daily work and the journey has been long and hard. But when I stand tall and let my heart lead me I am always okay and I feel hopeful.

Because there is always hope.

~Lisa Brown

When we allow it, grief leads us on a path of self- discovery.

~ Christine L. Bavarro LMHC

One Small Thing

I think my grief journey began in the months before my husband died. During that time as he became sicker and required my constant care, it was apparent to me that he was nearing the end. I buried my sadness and deep loss inside so that I would have the strength to support him emotionally and physically in every way that I could. I did not allow myself to think about his impending death so that I could immerse myself in his daily care. He kept telling me and my children he was worried about me. I thought I would be okay once the stress of his illness was over. I promised him I would be alright. Was I ever wrong.

After his death my family returned to their homes and lives. That's when the grief hit me. I realized I was alone without my partner, companion and listener. I could barely face each day. I couldn't eat, didn't care about anything and spent many days just lying on the couch, crying, missing him, feeling guilty, wishing I had done more. I didn't know how to live without him. I no longer had a purpose.

At first when I went to places we used to go I'd get sad seeing other couples holding hands and being together. But with the encouragement and support I received in my bereavement group I began to see my life differently. Instead of looking at my sad and alien life as a giant, insurmountable mountain, I began to break each day down into a series of smaller challenges. At first it would be just to try to do something for myself each day. It might be just sitting outside reading a book, going for a walk alone or with a friend, something small that was peaceful and pleasant.

Succeeding at each small challenge was gradually empowering. When I was able to accomplish one small thing that I felt good about doing alone, it would give me confidence to do another. I thought about the activities I once enjoyed and began to try them one at a time. When something felt good I would incorporate it into my life. This helped me to develop new resources, comforting habits and the ability to put myself first. My family had always come first before, but now it was appropriate and necessary to concentrate on myself. It was difficult, especially making decisions without him, but with each decision it got a little easier.

Now, a year and a half since my loss I am amazed and proud of how far I've come. He is always with me as I live each day, doing things one at a time. I am finding joy in each day and giving myself permission to heal. We had a beautiful life together and those memories are what give me hope that life can still be beautiful. I am sure he would not have wanted me to suffer as I did. But through the experience of profound loss, you learn that fully feeling it and moving through it brings you to the other side where a different life is waiting for you. You find your strength and realize how resilient you can be. That new life is a different life, but I'm finding, to my relief and surprise, that it is still a good life.

~ Carol

Till Death Do Us Part

"Till death do us part "... I never thought in a million years that Bob and I would experience "do us part" after just 28 years of marriage. This isn't the way we had it planned. Our children were growing up. We were planning our "empty nest years". Trips to be taken, weddings to plan, and of course becoming Grandparents.

But life has a way of happening while we're making other plans. "...I am sorry but you have cancer ". Hearing those ominous words changed the rhythm of our daily lives and put us on the single minded path of trying to treat Bob's cancer. But the prognosis wasn't good and my husband lost his courageous battle just 11 months after his diagnosis.

I was 49 years old and a widow...that word filled me with anxiety and made me wonder how I would survive without Bob. What would my children do without their dad? What would I do without my partner and best friend? Could I afford to stay in our home? I had no answers.

I fumbled my way through that first year of grief and despair. There was no blue print to follow. When I finally fell asleep at night I often dreamed of him. In those dreams he came to me and told me I would be fine and everything would be okay. But each morning I woke up wondering why I was still here to see the sunrise and Bob wasn't. I began to question every belief I'd ever had about spirituality and existence. The idea of dying so that I could be with Bob was something I thought about and even longed for. But you can't try out death to see what it's like. Death was final as I knew only too well.

This spiritual and emotional crisis became my whole existence. In my dark dis-function I ran back to the church for solace. Many days I sat in a pew alone just trying to feel comforted. "Please God help me feel better", I repeated like a prayer. I had forgotten what feeling good was like.

I believe that prayer was answered because not long after I found myself at a grief group which later led me to individual therapy. The group facilitator had experienced personal loss and had many suggestions to encourage us to try to help slowly build a new life. "What are your dreams?" she asked. My dreams? I had always lived life as part of a couple and my dreams were part of the life we shared together. Now I was being told to begin again, to search my heart for new meaning and direction.

It was countless baby steps that helped me start to rebuild my life. Each step I took brought me to more solid ground where I could examine new interests and try out new possibilities ...like getting involved in photography. Picking up my camera has had the biggest impact of all. It has helped me heal my broken heart and anguished soul. It has renewed my spirit and restored my faith in the world. With each click a feeling of energy runs through me. As I look through the camera lens I see the wonder and beauty of the world around me. I see Bob in every beautiful landscape and feel his love in every sunset I capture on film. I feel his presence as though he is wrapping his arms around me, and I smile as I remember my dreams when he would come to me and tell me everything would be okay.

Bob's journey here on earth was complete, of that I am sure. He accomplished everything he set out to do and fulfilled his dreams. It is my job to complete mine. I don't question anymore why I get to wake up each morning...I have lots to do.

~ Helen Cogan

Living and Loving

I remember being told by people several months after David's death, "Patti in time you will heal, your pain won't be as bad, and someday you will even meet someone and marry again." I was appalled by this and wondered how in God's name these people could know these things to be true! I had just lost my soul mate of whom I had been with since the age of sixteen and they wanted me to believe that it would get better? I was having none of it. I knew my life had changed as I had known it and that it would never be the same again. Furthermore I didn't want it to get better nor did I ever want to meet someone new! I felt I was destined to live my life alone, after all who could ever replace the love of my life. Time passed, our eldest son Marc had gotten married and was trying very hard to start his new life, while our youngest son Matthew and I continued trying to run the family business. After a while, he wanted to go out on his own moving in with some buddies, and although I knew it was time for him to make his own way, I was scared to death of his leaving. At the age of 47 I would find myself on my own for the first time in my life. I had gone from my parent's home to making a home with David. This was one of the many secondary losses I would come to experience, as if losing my husband hadn't been enough! So on that day, as I stood at the window watching him put the last of his things in his truck, trying very hard not to burst into tears, I heard David's voice say "it's time hon, don't worry you both will be okay" and although I didn't quite believe it, I knew he was right and that it was time for us both to make our way into this unknown world of what was to be.

After some time, of being on my own and still running the heating business I decided to volunteer at hospice. They had given such wonderful care to David, and I felt it would be a way of showing my appreciation. This changed my life. I was drawn to those who were bereaved and soon found myself working in the bereavement dept. I went back to school and received my Thanatology certificate, and realized this work was what I was meant to do. Ironic really to think that my beloved husband had to die for me to be in this place doing the work that I so love to do.

My life had changed so much, but there was something missing, laughter. David had always made me laugh, actually enjoyed doing it and I missed that. So, on a sunny day in August I met someone who made me laugh again. I realized that my heart was big enough to love and be loved again and that by doing so,it would never mean that I hadn't love David. In fact nothing could be further from the truth. I will always hold dear and never forget the love and the memories of what we shared together. But I have found while on this grief journey that the way for me to honor David's memory is to live my life and make meaning of it, and I hear his voice telling me "it's okay hon" and now I believe it!

~ Patti Comeau-Simonson

"Hope is faith holding out its hand in the dark."

George Isles

Everything Will Be Okay

"Mommy do that again!" My three young children squealed from the back seat as my station wagon splashed through the flooded streets nearly engulfing us and obliterating my view of the road ahead. I gripped the wheel in fear, struggling to navigate us safely through this violent rain storm without betraying my panic to the kids. What was I thinking being out here on this winding country road several miles from home? Why wasn't Craig here when I needed him? And how can my kids actually be laughing and enjoying this frightening excursion as though it was a Disney ride?

Barely two months had passed since the nightmarish August day that changed our lives forever. That morning began as a perfect summer day filled with the promise of tea parties and finger painting on the back porch. Instead a stone faced police officer pulled up to my house and informed me that my husband Craig had been in a serious car accident on his way to work and was killed instantly. My beautiful, loving husband of 18 years, my childhood sweetheart, my rock, my best friend, and the light of my life was suddenly and irretrievably gone. I soon learned that no amount of disbelief or pleading would bring him back. Darkness fell like a shroud on my new reality, burying all my hopes and dreams.

The kids felt the loss too, deeply and fiercely, often waking in the night in tears of rage as though rediscovering the awful truth that Daddy really was gone. And I in my sheer emotional and physical exhaustion could only numbly hold them until sleep mercifully overtook them, murmuring that everything would be okay, and wishing I believed it.

But mostly during the day they were incredibly elastic little creatures, able to feel joy in the moment they were in. They could swing on their swings as high as the clouds, race each other around the yard, and enjoy every chance they got to laugh and dance and run. They could bounce like little rubber balls and I envied that ability.

The car continued down the road, the wheels spraying great walls of water as I listened to my children's happy sounds. The laughter and joy they were experiencing seemed to chip away at the thick walls of sorrow I surrounded myself with. As we neared our destination the heavy rains began to subside and the skies began to brighten off to our left. I breathed a grateful sigh of relief, feeling the slightest bit hopeful that we would survive this ride, when my oldest daughter shouted excitedly, "Look Mommy! There's a rainbow!" The four of us looked to see the most amazing sight...a perfectly arched rainbow hanging across the sky, its colorful brightness surpassing any rainbow I'd ever seen before.

The sky was still churning with storm clouds, except for this one beautiful section that had opened above us. The clouds surrounding the rainbow were filled with billowing, celestial light as though Heaven itself had flung open its doors and sent down rays of hope. I pulled the car over to take in this rare and unexpected visual treat. Following a sacred moment of wonder and awe, my four year old son reverently asked, "Mommy, is that what Heaven looks like?" Before I could answer, my six year old daughter explained in a voice filled with unwavering faith "Of course that's what Heaven looks like Seth! Daddy is there now, and he sent us this rainbow." "Did he Mommy?" my oldest asked. Suddenly I was overwhelmed with the pure openness and innocence of my children's hearts and this sweet moment of grace that had been sent to us. And I knew exactly what to say. "I think Daddy sent us this beautiful rainbow so that we would know that he's always thinking of us. And to tell us that everything will be okay." And in that one perfect moment I came to believe it.

~ Deborah Wile-Taves

The journey of a thousand miles must
Begin with a single step.

~Lao Tzu, Ancient Chinese Philosopher

Love Conquers All

In January 2009, Scooby was surrendered to the animal shelter by his heartbroken owner. Shortly thereafter Scooby became my foster dog. I created an ad to re-home him, writing, "Scooby is a ten year old chocolate lab. While he is overweight, he is seemingly healthy. He is housebroken and up to date on all of his vaccinations. He is such a friendly dog that I want to rename him "HAPPY". He gets along with both dogs and cats." Scooby was soon adopted by a lovely retired couple. They were an ideal home for him. Despite this, after I dropped Scooby off there, I cried for the entire ride home.

Scooby thrived in his new home. He comforted the wife whose health was declining from Alzheimer's, provided the husband with an enthusiastic walking companion and was also playfully entertaining to all he met. The wife passed away in mid- 2011 and Scooby continued to provide companionship to the husband until January 2013 when the husband began having mobility issues and could no longer care for Scooby. So, Scooby came back to live with me again. While older and grey in the muzzle, he retained his gregarious, stereotypical lab like personality. No matter what the circumstances Scooby approached life with enthusiasm, evidenced by his rocking horse type run and his vibrant tail wagging. I continued his "HAPPY" nickname since it was so well suited to his nature.

Scooby passed away on November 11, 2014. He was held by me and a friend from doggie daycare who loved him very much – each of us with red eyes and tears streaming down our faces – as he took his final breaths. While I initially thought that the final grief was mine alone, I was completely mistaken. He touched the hearts of many. Friends near and far sent condolences. A donation was made to the animal shelter in his name. One of the most precious and comforting gifts I received came from Scooby's adoptive dad upon hearing of Scooby's passing:

"Thank you for your lovely card that told us that Scooby had died. He must have been about 15 years. He leaves a lot of people who were glad that they knew him and sad that he is gone. My son, and his two kids shed a few tears when they heard. Scooby was especially fond of my son. There were also a few neighbors who helped me with him. They were sad when you took him and now sad that he is gone. I used the word "sad" many times. But actually we all benefited from knowing him. There is a magic about a good dog that is certainly due to the fact people and dogs evolved together. Dogs may be the only animal in the world that actually loves another species better than its own."

I was supported in my grief with love. And in the end, love conquers all.

~ Joan Mulloney Stone

"Hope to me means a possible light at the end of the tunnel and a belief that things will get better with time."

Sarah, peer facilitator

Reminders of Love

I remember, on the day I buried my wife, standing by the hearse and looking up to see a commercial airliner leaving a contrail in the sky. From my perspective its angle appeared very steep and I recall viewing it as my wife's soul on its way to heaven.

Months of grief, despair, and hopelessness followed. I would often take long walks on a beach my wife and I had frequented and talk to her to ease my distress. On one such day when I was feeling particularly hopeless, I asked her, as I walked the beach, to help me just get through the day. A short time later my attention was caught by a brilliant contrail streaking across a clear blue sky toward the horizon. I felt that she had answered me in the only way she could. My despair lifted and hope was restored.

I no longer associate contrails with my wife's death. They are now gifts from her, reminders of her love, and symbolize for me progress toward a brighter future.

~ Craig Daley

"Hope is the greatest treasure you have. When all else fails, it is something to hang onto"

Patti, peer facilitator

Facing Grief

Grief (n): deep sorrow caused especially by someone's death.

It is easiest for me to think of grief as a word, a noun, something tangible and something rational. When my father, Robert, passed away I was 21, and I hung on to what, to me, was rational and true. My dad would always speak in absolutes, which during his life I hated, and then I so quickly needed. I needed a black and white view of those sad days to get through them. Dad had cancer. Dad was getting better. Dad was getting worse. Dad has died.

I first approached grief cautiously and with reason, but grief is smart and defies reason. I tried to rationalize death and mortality, because like most juniors in college I thought I was the smartest person in the room. If I could just reason my way out of grief, I could escape. In those days leading up to, and shortly after, his passing, defying grief gave me strength. I needed this strength then, to hand out to my mother and to lend a shoulder for the tears of my sister. But grief is persistent and relentless, and was slow to back down.

For me grief has not been something to get over, but to get through. Even now grief is always there, in the background of a family photo or in the corner of a memory. Just days after being diagnosed with cancer my father flew to Rome to visit me during a semester in Italy. We trekked through the ancient capital lighting candles in what felt like every church, and praying together, wordlessly, for health and happiness. It is one of my favorite memories of my father. There is a photo of him I took in front of a shop window, I am not sure what it was advertising, but the photo is my father standing in front of angel wings with arms outstretched, smiling. It is when I look at this photo that I acknowledge grief, and just for a moment I allow grief in.

It took letting grief in for me to know that it cannot be out smarted. I found that if I let grief in, just for a second, I could think of my dad and remember the good times we had together. I could remember how he would always leave these long, pointless voicemails about his day and asking me about an exam or a class. It is at that instant that I look at grief and laugh. I smile at grief and enjoy the moment of happiness that it brought with its sadness.

The way that I now deal with grief is to confront it, because you cannot out run grief. By facing grief head on I am able to move forward, and to get through the sorrow together with my wife, my family, and the memories of my father.

~Shawn Cogan

"Hope is where you go, deep into your heart and soul to find a place that is safe and loving. It has the ability to help us rise to any occasion in our lives. It is that breathe of fresh air that greets us at our most difficult times."

Helen, peer facilitator

Hope Emerges

I will never forget that clear, chilly morning of April 9, 2005 when Mary Ann died. As I walked down the concourse of Salem Hospital, from the Hospice unit, loneliness and desolation consumed me. Phone calls had been made to my son and mother-in-law, but the most daunting moment was still ahead.

When I arrived home to share the tragic news, my younger daughter, Tricia, through tears, said "…but I only had her for twenty years."   No words could temper that. Hope seemed lost.

Hope emerged that same year with my son Tim's marriage and it flourished with the arrival of my granddaughter Nora. Oh, what a joy!

One day when Nora was three, I noticed her staring at a portrait of Mary Ann, commissioned by Hospice of the North Shore, that hangs in my living room. Noticing her childhood innocence and curiosity, I said, "Nora, that is the Nana who loved you before you were born."

When Mary Ann's breast cancer had returned with a vengeance after two years of chemo and radiation, a dear friend sent her a painting of a rose with a note that said, " Mary Ann, you are like a rose that grows up into the sky toward the sunlight and now God has you in his sight."

That thought inspired me. In her eulogy I concluded as follows:

"You know for the past few days it seems to me that our sky has been a much more vivid blue. I think I know why. Feel safe! Mary Ann is now keeping all of us in her sight."

Last year I walked the beach at Good Harbor in Gloucester as I do every year on April 9th. It was Mary Ann's favorite place. That day the ocean was angry, the surf roaring, the wind biting and the sky covered with a thick layer of clouds. As I was departing, heading toward the beach house, I looked back over my shoulder. Suddenly, a bright ray of sunshine pierced the clouds and reflected off the ocean.

It is true.

Mary Ann does have us in her sight!

~ Ray Donnelly

Grief changes us

The pain Sculpts us

into someone Who

Understands more deeply

Hurts more often

Appreciates more quickly

Cries more easily

Hopes more desperately

Loves more openly

~unknown

Before and After

The loss of a child…unimaginably agonizing, deeply sorrowful, heartbreakingly devastating. Nothing, including the death of my husband 20 years earlier prepared me for the death of my son, Jordan. It had always seemed to me that the role of mothering is meant to withstand time, and to have the mortal bond between mother and son broken so prematurely left me feeling utterly shattered.

Some spoke of staying hopeful. The concept of hope for the future seemed laughable-I hadn't yet signed on for living. I teetered on the precipice between normal grief and insanity for what seemed to be an immeasurable amount of time. When did hope sneak in? Perhaps it happened when I finally understood that my grief would not kill me despite how powerless and frightened I was feeling. Or, maybe it was once I accepted that my life would always be divided into "before" and "after" with the split occurring the morning of the visit from the Army chaplain and the city police officer. However it began, it was subtle, almost imperceptible. Hope began to flicker for brief moments in the shadows, flashes that just as quickly vanished. I noticed that my sorrow slowly became incorporated into my daily life and no longer seemed insurmountable. It has been said that without hope, there is no possibility of happiness. And, living a life without any happiness at all seems inconceivable. I chose hope.

Five years later, I see bereaved parents as part of my private psychotherapy practice. It's easy to recognize the now-familiar raw, wounded look in their eyes as they walk in to my office. "Tell me about your child," I say and we begin to work together with a mutual understanding about the massive crack in their hearts and their need for solace and comfort. Briefly I think of Jordan and about how my love for him lives on in a way neither of us could have predicted. Then my client and I proceed, step by step in aching emotional proximity. We talk about sons and daughters, about grief and despair and then later about hope and healing. All the while I think about how hope for my own future was born out of a longing to live my life in a way that my son would be as proud of me as I am of him.

~ Holly Shay

"Hope is the inspiration to open closed doors and explore new paths."

Ray, peer facilitator

A Mother's Love

It's been almost 2 and ½ years since I lost my mom to cancer. She was my best friend, my role model, my North Star. We had an uncommonly close and loving relationship that was a constant source of strength in my life. We enjoyed each other's company and loved spending time together, going to movies and concerts, going shopping and to restaurants, playing games, and just hanging out. It never occurred to me that she would die so soon, before I married and before I had children. The void her death created hit me hard and left me rudderless and adrift. The future seemed empty and joyless without her.

Though I had the help of my loving family, my fiancé, my support group and my friends, I often felt so alone, filled with the longing and sadness. Somehow I knew I had to create a life without her, but I also needed to feel close to her, to feel that loving connection we'd always had. So I made a simple decision to continue our weekly Wednesday lunches. Every Wednesday I brought a chair to the cemetery where I would sit at her grave and eat my lunch. Maybe it was the peacefulness, or taking the time to close my eyes and rest, but I felt close to her there. The connectedness I felt soothed my soul. Those weekly lunches soon increased to several times a week, and then every day. The ritual was comforting and gave me a new way that I could be with my mother. I even began including my now husband for one breakfast each weekend. I instinctively nurtured myself the way my mother had always nurtured me, with patience, unconditional love and acceptance. I gave myself the time and space I needed to heal.

Every day since her death I have worn a necklace that belonged to her. It has a charm that has her name written in Hawaiian, and I added a favorite ring with a rose on it. Whenever I am feeling anxious or upset I hold the necklace and slide the ring on and off my fingers. It's like she is there with me, giving me comfort.

One of the hardest challenges I had to face was to get married without her there. But by now I knew that our connection was unbreakable and I would find many ways to include her spirit. I used fabric from the dress she wore to my sister's wedding in my wedding dress. I included her favorite Hawaiian plumerias in my flowers, and I made a photo collage for the ceremony. My husband and I danced to Carrie Underwood's song "Mamma's Song", I wore some of her jewelry, and I tied her wedding rings to my bouquet. I honored her with a donation to the kidney cancer foundation in lieu of favors. Her beautiful spirit was in every detail and I felt stronger than I ever thought I could be.

As I embark on the next chapter of my life and start a family of my own I know it is going to be difficult without my mom's physical presence to guide and advise me. But I have learned that I can continue to include her in this endeavor as well. If I have a daughter, she will be given my mom's name as her middle name. My child will find comfort in a baby blanket my mother had made, and I've started a scrapbook about her to give to my children. They will come to know how special she was and how many lives she touched.

When I think about my mom, I think about all the good times I had with her, and how much I am like her. I learned so much from her, how to love and care for others, how to be a good listener, how to cook and make a loving home. I am the woman I am today because of her, and I hope to be the type of wife and mother she was. She remains an amazing gift in my life and I will hold her in my heart forever.

~ Sarah Chipman

A Journey of Love

The day our grieving began there was no death in the physical sense of someone dying, but it was the day my beautiful, healthy, and fit wife Elizabeth, was diagnosed with a brain tumor that our lives were changed forever. I have discovered that grief doesn't begin for everyone upon the passing of your loved one. Rather it begins when everything you knew as your "normal" is thrown into chaos. Disbelief, fear and anger crowd your mind and vie for control over the Faith and Hope you have for a cure. The innocence by which you lived your life with dreams for the future is replaced by the knowledge that each moment is precious and not to be squandered.

The day after her diagnosis I walked into my church and sobbed at the alter stairs, begging for a mistake in diagnosis. This was the church I had come to daily to meditate for the past 10 years, where both Liz and I had been christened, married, and where our children had been baptized. Surely I could bargain for a miracle here in exchange for my undying faith.

As we numbly began to formulate our medical plan of attack, I went into overdrive in the role of caregiver; protective, nurturing, supportive. During quiet moments I blanketed in grief. There was one instance where I was waiting in the examining room with Liz and not even realizing I was shaking my head in reaction to the thoughts running through my head. Liz asked me why I was shaking my head. I told her that at that moment I could name 100 people that needed a life lesson and that we did not need this lesson. Disgust was evident in my tone, and in typical Liz fashion she responded, "Why do you think I should be exempt? No one is exempt Dana! It is my journey and we will deal with it."

Her strength always astounded me, but moments of self- pity and denial continued to plague me. I remember sitting in the waiting room at Dana Farber where hundreds gathered daily to receive and monitor their progress and I again went dark. Looking around I silently muttered that we didn't belong here, we shouldn't be here with these people, as if they were somehow responsible for us being there. And suddenly I heard a voice from somewhere shout at me, "Wake up Dana! None of these people belong here, not one of them wants to be here." It is in that moment that I had my epiphany and transitioned from denial to empathy, from feeling victimized to having compassion for all of us.

With the courage Liz showed us, the children and I endeavored for the next three years to journey with her, attend every treatment, every follow-up appointment, every MRI, in the same spirit as she did, with Faith, Hope and Courage. We channeled our sadness into cherishing every moment we had with her. We said the things we needed to say to each other and did the things we wanted to do. Our God blessed us with grace in that the tumor did not compromise Liz's ability to walk, talk or communicate…a gentler form of brain cancer than afflicts some.

Liz entered hospice at the Kaplan house where she spent the last week of her life. My children and I filled her room with reminders of the wonderful family life we built together. My son and I read her the story of the Dragonfly, giving Liz some quiet pleasure as she had always had a passion for the dragonfly. On the last day that Liz was truly conscious, I buried my head in her lap and sobbed. Even though she had no strength to speak, she stroked my hand to give me comfort. Facing her own mortality she was still teaching me about grace, acceptance and love as she had done all of our married life.

Liz died in my arms, just she and I, alone in the room. All week I had anticipated this moment with dread, thinking that I would experience desperate loneliness at her passing. Instead it was the most beautiful and intimate moment for both of us, for it ended just as it had begun 27 years before, in each other's arms.

My journey since Elizabeth's death has been filled with the feelings of grief. But there have also been moments of illumination, hard won wisdom and hope for the future. Our children are thriving and they inspire me with the resilience of youth. It is through them that I realize that life, love and laughter is JOY in itself, and I am reminded to not take one single moment for granted. I am so incredibly grateful for my time with Elizabeth and the beautiful life we shared. Whatever the future holds, I will always be inspired by the miracle that she was to me, knowing that love lives on forever.

~ Dana Markos

The Bridge of Healing

I've come to think of grieving as a long, healing bridge that leads those of us who are mourning to a place of transformation, acceptance and peace.

When my brother Terrence died of suicide at age 49, I knew that I would never be the same. I also knew that I would never be able to go back in time. I would need to somehow move forward and keep living, one day, one hour, one minute at a time. Each activity of remembrance and every gesture of sympathy and even crying would help me to inch along this bridge of healing to a new place in my life.

Eight years later, I'm still on that bridge. The grief, of course, never goes away, but it does change and I can feel over time that I am a little further along that bridge. I still wish that there were things I could go back in time and change but this journey doesn't allow us to go backwards or to turn back the clock.

I don't know how I got through those first weeks after he died. I didn't think I would survive his funeral. I literally felt like my heart would either stop beating or would implode with grief. I remember the feeling of loss and tragedy and mourning to be so crushing and heavy that it took every ounce of strength to even get dressed, to drive, to make dinner for my children. Once I even realized that my pants were on inside out while I was at the grocery store.

A few months after Terrence died, I wanted to come up with a meaningful way to keep his memory alive. I also wanted to help others with their grief if possible. Helping others has always been a way for me to "get out of my own head" and to possibly brighten someone else's moments of darkness. Maybe if I could help alleviate someone else's suffering, it would help alleviate some of mine.

These tandem needs provided the inspiration for an idea that changed my life. I called it The Forever Bracelet because even though my brother was physically gone from this earth and that nothing I could do would bring him back, I took some comfort over time in knowing that he would be forever in my memories... forever in my heart.

The Forever Bracelet includes symbols of loss but also of hope and transformation including a teardrop, a butterfly and a heart engraved with the word "Forever." When I wear my Forever Bracelet it gives me a chance to remember my brother, to talk to him in my thoughts, and at times to tell others about him. It is a source of comfort and strength. I think he would like knowing that the proceeds of sales of The Forever Bracelet go to hospice and bereavement charities...that something good in some way came from this terrible tragedy of his life ending too soon.

Everyone's bridge of healing will look different. The things that might help you move a tiny bit forward on your bridge of healing might be very different than the things that I found helpful. There's no right way...no timeline, no deadlines...just tiny steps forward across a bridge of healing and hope that leads you to somewhere new.

~ Kathy Ridgely Beal

Endings are also Beginnings
The world is round and the place
which may seem like the end
may also be only the beginning.

~ Ivy Baker Priest,
American politician

Bibliography

Allen Klein, Learning to Laugh When You Feel Like Crying
                Embracing Life after Loss
Goodman Beck Publishing, 2011

Christine Lalli Bavaro, LMHC with Anne Elise O'Connor
                    Moving through Loss
Universe Inc. New York, 2009

Helen Cogan; helencoganphotography.com

Patti Comeau-Simonson; hopeandhealingpeers.com

Deborah Wile-Taves editor; wile_taves@verizon.net

About the Authors

Patti Comeau-Simonson first worked in hospice care as a volunteer. After receiving her Thanatology certificate, she continued working in bereavement. Through her own personal loss she has resolved to use that experience to help others with similar losses by creating Hope and Healing with Peers Training and Support Program. She feels that peers can offer valuable support to those who have lost a loved one simply because the peers have "lived the experience." Patti has trained many peer facilitators who then go on to lead peer led support groups for those who wish to continue the next level of their journey. These "Hope Representatives" offer living proof that people do heal and are able to find Hope again. Patti continues to provide education and speaks regularly at the Hospice & Palliative Care Federation of Massachusetts.

Helen Cogan's husband lost his courageous battle to cancer in 2009 which prompted her to pick up her camera as she tried to heal her broken heart. Through photographing the world around her, she has found an enormous amount of gratitude for life. After participating in a bereavement support group she then trained to become a peer facilitator. She continues to companion those who have lost a loved one, helping them to find hope again.

Made in the USA
Charleston, SC
30 May 2015